educating *your* child

... its not rocket science!

Dr Kevin Donnelly

Published in 2012 by Connor Court Publishing Pty Ltd.

Copyright © Kevin Donnelly 2012

ALL RIGHTS RESERVED. This book contains material protected under International and Federal Copyright Laws and Treaties. Any unauthorized reprint or use of this material is prohibited. No part of this book may be reproduced or transmitted in any form or by any means, electronic or mechanical, including photocopying, recording, or by any information storage and retrieval system without express written permission from the publisher.

Connor Court Publishing Pty Ltd.
PO Box 1
Ballan VIC 3342
sales@connorcourt.com
www.connorcourt.com

ISBN: 9781921421730 (pbk.)

Cover design by Ian James

Printed in Australia

Contents

1. INTRODUCTION: EDUCATION BEGINS IN THE HOME   1

2. THE DIGITAL AGE: GOOD OR BAD?   11

3. GROUND HELICOPTER PARENTS & LET CHILDREN TAKE RISKS   19

4. BACK TO BASICS   27

5. CHILDREN NEED A MORAL COMPASS   35

6. CULTURAL LITERACY: WHAT ALL CHILDREN SHOULD KNOW   43

7. HOW TO CHOOSE THE RIGHT SCHOOL   53

8. COPING WITH BULLYING   61

9. PARENTS, TEACHERS AND SCHOOLS: IT'S A PARTNERSHIP   67

10. UNDERSTANDING EDUCATION FADS AND JARGON   71

11. CONCLUSION   79

1
Introduction: Education Begins in the Home

Now, we all know that schools can't do it alone. As parents, the task begins at home. It begins by turning off the TV and helping with homework, and encouraging a love of learning from the very start of our children's lives. And I'm speaking from experience now. (Laughter). Malia and Sasha would often rather be watching American Idol *or* Sponge Bob, *but Michelle and I know that our first job, our first responsibility, is instilling a sense of learning, a sense of a love of learning in our kids. And so there are no shortcuts there; we have to do that job. And we can't just blame teachers and schools if we're not instilling that commitment, that dedication to learning, in our kids.*
President Obama, extract from a speech on NCLB Waivers, Flexibility, The White House, 23 September 2011.

As parents, the most precious gift we can give our children is a good education.

While a safe and loving home is important, it's education that will decide your children's future life and happiness.

A good education will teach your children the difference between right and wrong and how to live and work with others; a good education will help them discover what they are best at and what they most enjoy; a good education will lead to future careers and teach how to gain the most from life.

As a famous Australian politician once said, "life wasn't meant to be easy", and a good education also helps to deal with and overcome life's challenges, reversals and disappointments.

As parents, we understand the importance of learning and it's only natural that we want the best for our children.

But, what is the best?

- What is the best way to teach children to be resilient and to help them be confident and strong?
- What is the best way to teach children the difference between right and wrong?
- What is the best way to teach children how to read?
- Should memorising times tables be compulsory?
- Are open classrooms the best or should children work by themselves sitting at a desk?
- Single sex or co-education – what is the best for your child?
- Should children be told that they have failed or is it harmful and bad for their self-esteem?
- Are all children the same or do they need different types of schools and different types of learning experiences?
- Are computers, the internet, e-books and Game-Boys the best way to learn or do the new technologies harm children and teach bad habits?

The world we live in, and in which children are growing up is a very different one from what we, as parents, experienced when we were children. The new technologies have spread like wildfire over the last 40 years or so with computers, the internet, mobile phones and social networking sites like Facebook radically changing the way we communicate, are entertained and how we do business and interact with the wider world. While there are many benefits, there is also the downside of children being cyber bullied, wasting hours surfing the net and living in a virtual world devoid of human contact and face-to-face engagement.

Family life is more difficult and challenging with fewer couples getting married, higher rates of separation and divorce, greater financial pressure on families and many of our cities becoming congested, stressful to live in and less neighbourhood friendly.

From an early age, children are bombarded with advertising on radio and TV, on the web and at the movies and much of popular entertainment promotes ever increasing cycles of consumption, materialism and keeping up with the latest trend or fad.

Education is also no longer simple and straightforward.

If parents are confused about the best way to educate their children, then so are many teachers and education experts.

Every week, there are debates in the media and within our teacher training institutions about what is the best way to teach, about whether literacy and numeracy standards are better or worse, whether new technology helps or hinders learning, about the impact of bullying and poor classroom discipline and the best way to fund government and non-government schools.

As a parent and someone who taught for 18 years in government and non-government secondary schools, teaching English and Politics, and who has been involved in education in Australia and overseas since 1975, even I find it difficult to keep up with debates and the ever changing fads.

This book is designed to help answer the above questions and to help parents make the right decisions. When it comes to your child's education, there is no second chance and mistakes can last a lifetime. It's also true that education opens the door to a world of learning that can excite and reward and, if done properly, provide a lifetime of opportunities, happiness and fulfilment.

10 commandments for parents (in no particular order)

1. Say 'no' to children and teach them respect and self-control.

2. Always have dinner at the table and make sure TVs, computers, Game-Boys, electronic readers and mobile phones are turned off (and no computers in the bedroom).
3. Surround children with myths, fables, legends, music, creative and practical arts.
4. Let children take risks and give them the space to make mistakes.
5. Give children a moral compass that will help them decide right from wrong.
6. Respect teachers and support schools in educating your child.
7. Understand that every child is different.
8. Understand that you cannot live your child's life.
9. Realise that you are your child's first teacher.
10. Enjoy and love being a parent – there is nothing that will ever equal the experience.

(1) Why parents are important

While it is true that teachers and schools have a vital role to play in a child's education, parents and what happens in the home are equally, if not more, important.

What parents do and don't do is especially important during the first 4 to 5 years of growing up, the time before children go to kindergarten and on to primary school. During these early years children develop at an amazing rate, physically, emotionally and mentally and what they learn establishes the foundation on which their school education will be built.

It should not surprise that one of the indicators of whether a child will do well at school or not is the number of books in the home and whether parents have spent time reading to their children. Parents also have an important role to play in teaching their children to be civil to others, to respect older people, especially teachers, and to appreciate that learning requires effort, concentration and discipline.

When at school, there is still a role for parents. Whether making sure children have a quiet place to study, turning off the computers and TV to make sure they are not wasting time or teaching their children good manners, a parent's job is never finished. Ask teachers about what worries them the most about their job and causes the greatest trouble and stress and they will say it's badly behaved, rude students who have never been taught to sit still and focus on getting something done or to understand that they are not the centre of the universe.

The early years

Some experts say that pregnant mothers, as it is good for their unborn child, should listen to music. It's certainly true that babies in the womb feel stress and anxiety and that if the mother is upset and distressed this impacts on the child. In the first few years experts also say that in addition to being warm, loved, hugged and well-fed babies need colourful and stimulating surroundings in which to play and grow. Even before they can talk and understand language children are like blotting paper, soaking up everything around them and discovering and learning at a tremendous rate. While they obviously need to sleep and rest, babies also need to interact with an environment that engages them by introducing new experiences, sights, movement and sounds.

Babies love colour, shapes, sounds and music, they need to have:

- a colourful, bright, happy room with friezes or pictures on the walls – like Peter Rabbit, the Gumnut babies, jungle and animal themes or themes from nature,
- musical boxes to listen to and colourful cut outs and mobiles above their cots,
- a range of baby toys and rattles to hold and touch, and
- parents also should play music for babies to listen to and talk and

interact with them regularly. Even though it takes time for a child to learn how to use language, all that baby talk is important. It's only by parents talking to their baby, explaining what is happening around them and creating conversation that babies begin to understand language and start to communicate.

The world of the imagination

As children grow older they need a steady diet of nursery rhymes, fairy stories, myths, legends and classic tales from writers like the Brothers Grimm and Hans Christian Andersen. Nursery rhymes introduce children to the musical and poetic quality of language as well as being enjoyable for their own sake. Tales like those from *Aesop's Fables* introduce children to important moral questions like the difference between right and wrong and what is the best way to treat others.

While written many years ago stories like *The Emperor's New Clothes* teach us how a child's innocence and honesty can see through the conceit and foolishness of elders and *The Goose that Laid the Golden Egg* shows us that being greedy can be very short sighted as it often leads to destroying what is most valuable.

Reading bed time stories also provides time for parents and their children to spend time together after a busy day and to share the enjoyment and excitement of entering a world of the imagination. It's no secret that many families now rely on both parents working to make ends meet and bedtime stories provide time out to re-establish contact and to forge the bonds that make family life such a joy.

Early Greek, Roman and Norse myths, legends and stories are also an important part of our cultural heritage and films like *Troy* and *The Clash of the Titans* prove how popular and enduring such stories are hundreds of years after they were first spoken or written. The American child psychologist Bruno Bettelheim also argues that myths, fables and legends are important for children's emotional and psychological development. In such stories children learn about anger and grief, jealousy and pride and how to overcome adversity and conquer fear.

Best illustrated by the "Star Wars" films by George Lucas, stories of heroes battling against adversity and treachery never go out of date. The conflict between good and evil, and conflicting emotions, like fear and courage and loyalty and betrayal, are always with us and it's important that children are introduced to them and begin to understand human nature and what drives people to act the way they do.

Examples of nursery rhymes, fairy tales, myths and legends and picture books that we read to our two children, James and Amelia, include:

- nursery rhymes like *Old Mother Hubbard*, *The Old Women who Lived in a Shoe*, *This Little Pig Went to Market*, *The Owl and the Pussy-cat*, *Little Jack Horner;*
- fairy tales like *Snow White*, *Sinbad the Sailor*, *Little Red Riding Hood*, *Jack and the Beanstalk*, *The Frog Prince*, *Cinderella*, *Prince Omar and Princess Scheherazade*, *Sleeping Beauty*, *Blue Beard* and *Tom Thumb;*
- myths, legends and stories from different cultures and lands, including the *Iliad* and the *Odyssey*, *Tales from Olympus*, *Pandora's Box*, *Narcissus*, *Romulus and Remus*, *The Grendel*, *The Stolen Hammer of Thor*, *The Monkey Who Would be King*, Kipling's *The Jungle Book* and *Queen Boadicea;*
- modern picture books that introduce children to print and fun stories like *Spot the Dog*, *Who Sank the Boat?*, *The Jolly Postman*, *Peepo*, *Angelina Ballerina*, *Tiddalick*, *Mr Little's Noisy Car* and picture books like *Animalia* and *Where's Wally?*

Painting, drawing, music, shapes, discovering the world of numbers and learning to read

During the early years and before going to school it is important that parents take time to introduce their children to a broad range of games and educational activities. Spending time with young children not only strengthens the bonds of love and affection, it also helps children to be in a better position to cope with the early years of kindergarten and primary school. Activities should include:

- playing with brightly coloured building blocks,
- finger painting and cutting and pasting shapes and cut outs,
- playing with simple musical instruments like recorders, trumpets, xylophones, tambourines and drums,
- playing with plasticine and play dough and learning how to paint,
- learning to build and make things with lego and meccano,
- playing with number games and beginning to recognise, count and subtract simple numbers, and
- playing games that teach children to memorise what has gone before and correctly guessing what will come next.

When at school

For many mothers, one of the hardest days they have to face is when their young loved one heads off to school for the first time. For other mothers, the day cannot come soon enough! Whatever your experience, even though children have begun school there is still a lot that parents can do to support teachers and to make sure their child's educational experience is a successful one. Parents need to:

- teach their children how to sit still, work quietly and concentrate on the task at hand. Children who do whatever they want at home, are noisy and jump from activity to activity without ever

finishing anything are difficult to teach and they make it harder for other children to learn,
- share with their children the enjoyment and satisfaction that comes from mastering something difficult. Whether it's cooking, doing repairs around the house, playing a musical instrument, sewing or building a cubby house it's important to get children involved and to show them the enjoyment and benefits that come from persevering and doing a job well,
- teach their children respect for authority, good manners and how to be civil and polite to others. Young children are often self-centred and think that they should get whatever they want, when they want it – wrong! If schools and classrooms are to work successfully children must understand that they are a part of a learning community and that they should respect teachers and their classmates,
- understand that they should not always take their child's side when things go wrong at school. While there might be the odd occasion when teachers do get it wrong, for most of the time they are genuinely concerned with their students' well-being and teachers should be supported and given the benefit of the doubt,
- take their children to museums, art galleries, musical and other cultural events. At a time when the temptation for children and teenagers is to live in a virtual world of computer games, the internet, Game-Boys and to spend hours on social sites like Facebook, it's important for parents to introduce them to the wider, more enriching world of history, music, dance and art,
- help their children establish a routine that allows a proper balance between time-off, homework and study, enjoying time together as a family and socialising with friends,
- make sure that children have a quiet and comfortable place to study where they will not be distracted, interrupted or have the

chance to waste time surfing the net or playing computer games,
- monitor their children's learning during the early primary school years, especially with the basics like literacy and numeracy. While is unfair to push children too hard and to make unrealistic demands it is also important that any learning problems are identified and dealt with earlier rather than later,
- take on interest in what they are studying and without looking over their shoulders all the time and taking over, show that you are interested in what they are learning, and
- know when their children are adult enough to make their own decisions about what they want to study and their future education and careers.

2

The Digital Age: Good or Bad? Using the New Technologies

In 1984, when I was teaching in the western suburbs of Melbourne, I was one of the first teachers in Victoria to introduce computers into the classroom. As part of the English class, students wrote and edited their stories on screen and I was amazed how motivated they were and how much time and effort they put into their work.

I can still remember the excitement of buying my first Macintosh 128K computer and games like shuttlecock and, as the new technology developed, going on the world-wide-web for the first time. Since the early to mid-'90s I have used computers and the internet on a daily basis and as I sit typing this chapter into my fifth generation Macintosh (while checking emails, paying some bills, downloading research papers and Skyping friends) I realise the value of the new technologies and how useful they are.

Welcome to the global village

We live in a global village with instant communication around the world via television, computers, the internet, mobile phones and social networking sites like Facebook, Twitter and Skype. While parents are often described as out of date and old fashioned when it comes to new technology, children are celebrated as digital natives.

Schools have embraced the digital age and new technologies with a vengeance, including laptop computers, replacing printed books with e-books, making students use the internet to carry out research and getting them to create multi-modal texts. In some schools libraries have disappeared to be replaced by digital resource centres and classrooms transformed into open learning spaces where electronic whiteboards are used instead of blackboards, teachers are described as "guides by the side" and children become "knowledge navigators" surfing the net.

Homes have also been transformed and it's not just the number of TVs and the explosion in home theatres and 50 inch plus plasma and LCD TVs. A 2009 Australian Bureau of Statistics survey shows that computers and the internet are also taking over:

- 72% of households have internet access,
- 78% of households have a computer,
- between the years 1998 to 2008-09 internet use jumped from 16% to 72% and access to computers jumped 44% to 78%, and
- in a survey of 2.7 million children aged 5 to 14 years, 79% said they used the internet with home internet being the most common.

The new technologies – the way of the future

Just look at how schools market themselves and it's obvious that one of the key selling points is being at the cutting edge of new technology. Laptops are compulsory, electronic whiteboards are in every classroom and students learn the skills needed to surf the information super highway. It's not just schools, the Australian government is spending billions of dollars connecting schools and homes to the National Broadband Network and fulfilling its promise to provide computers to every senior school student.

One of the arguments used to defend investing in new technologies is that books are out of date. For hundreds of years we found knowledge, information and pleasure in reading the printed word – no longer! Today's students are techno-savvy and no longer read novels cover to cover. How many times do you see children as young as 6 and 7 in cafes playing with Game-Boys while their mum and dad sit drinking coffee? On public transport and walking through shopping centres, it looks as if every teenager has a mobile phone glued to his or her ear and having a site on Facebook is compulsory if you want to be part of the 'in' group at school.

The new technologies change the way we think

While nobody denies the value of computers, the internet and TV, for getting information, keeping in touch with friends and learning more about the world, the danger is that too much time on computer games, watching screens and surfing the net damages the way we process information and the way we think. Unlike printed texts that require you to focus on the words, concentrate, read carefully and sit quietly, TV and computer screens are full of colourful graphics, ever changing images, sounds and lots of movement.

When reading a printed page your eyes move from left to right following the words, with stops to process meaning, as you move systematically across and down the page. Reading a computer screen is very different as described by a US researcher, Jakob Nielson. Initially, reading a computer page is similar to reading a printed page, your eyes move from left to right in a methodical fashion but with computers, after a while, your eyes stop reading all the way across the screen and only read the left hand side – moving vertically instead of horizontally. Surfing the net is the opposite to reading a book as viewers, instead of reading page after page and working their way through each chapter, flit quickly from site to site and rarely spend more than a minute or two accessing information.

When is comes to the new technology, especially computer games, Professor Susan Greenfield from Oxford University puts it this way: "[The] environment has changed in an unprecedented way, it's bombarding you with boom, bang and bang images, what I call the 'yuck and wow' scenario where every moment you're having something flash up in your face and bombard your ear". Professor Greenfield, who specialises in researching how the human brain develops, is especially worried about the impact of TV and computers on young children.

The worst thing a parent can do, especially when they are toddlers, is to sit a child in front of a TV or let him or her play computer games for hours as being bombarded by sounds and ever changing, flickering images alters the way the young brain works. Professor Greenfield says, "My fear is that these technologies are infantilising the brain into the state of small children who are attracted by buzzing noises and bright lights, who have a small attention span and who live for the moment".

No wonder teachers complain that students are unable to sit still for long periods of time and work quietly. The reality is that if young children have never spent time reading a book or been taught that learning requires concentration and effort, everything at school will have to be designed to be immediately entertaining.

Computers and the internet stifle the imagination

Reading a novel or a poem requires concentration, weighing each word or sentence and using your imagination to enter the world created by the author or poet. We can all remember being so caught up when reading that it is almost as if we are there with the characters. You can be so engrossed that you don't even notice when somebody comes into the room or that you've been reading for so long. In the novel *To Kill a Mockingbird*, Atticus Finch tells his daughter that the best way to get to know someone is to get inside their skin and walk around in it. At its best reading the printed word, especially literature, allows that to happen as you live the lives of the characters, experiencing their emotions and feelings.

With computers and the internet students skim words and images, quickly moving from page to page and site to site without pausing.

Instead of enjoying the language and getting lost in what they are reading they are in the 'here and now' searching for information. Computers don't allow time to stop and think or promote the ability to reflect, the very things needed for a strong imagination and successful education.

Computers can dumb down learning

One of the arguments for using computers is that learning will improve. If only it were that simple! Research carried out analysing the results of international mathematics and science tests and examining why some countries and students do better than others suggests that computers hinder learning. The European researcher, Ludger Woessman, who carried out an investigation into the Programme for International Student Assessment (PISA) tests says, "... availability of computers at home is negatively related to student performance in maths and reading, and the availability of computers at school is unrelated to student performance".

Woessmann makes the point that students can waste time on computers and the internet (socialising, talking to friends, playing games) and he argues, "... availability of computers at home seems to distract students from learning". Research into how young children best learn also tells us that instead of relying on calculators and computers, students need to strengthen their brain power by memorising times tables, doing mental arithmetic and learning how to recite songs, ballads and poems by heart.

A couple of US studies into whether or not computers help disadvantaged students and the effectiveness of learning software programs also raise doubts about the new technology.

One study from Duke University examined the test scores and computer use of 150,000 primary age children and found that those children who didn't do well in the tests had high computer use with most of the time spent socialising and playing games. While governments across the world are spending billions making sure that more children have computers, the researchers conclude, "... programs to expand home computer access would lead to even wider gaps between test scores of advantaged and disadvantaged students".

A second US study examined the effectiveness of a number of educational software programs in helping students improve learning. In the US, as well as Australia, parents are spending millions of dollars ever year trying to give their child the edge by buying the latest education computer package. The US researchers, after evaluating the impact of a number of educational software products on classrooms, concluded, "Test scores were not significantly higher in classrooms using selected reading and mathematics software products".

It's understandable why computer companies and software designers advertise that the new technologies will raise standards and make students better learners, at the same time, parents need to be careful and make sure that whatever they spend money on has been proven to work.

New technologies – anti-social

New technologies take away valuable time from interacting with friends and family and learning how to deal with relationships face to face. An American researcher, David Putnam, some years ago wrote a book called *Bowling Alone* in which he argues that people no longer socialise and meet with others as they once did. One reason why sporting clubs and community groups have declined, he argues, is because of TV and the fact that most nights families get their entertainment at home. It's not unusual now for Australian families to have two to three TVs and a number of computers and laptops with children and teenagers disappearing into their bedrooms for hours every night caught up in a virtual world devoid of any real human contact.

There is also the problem that a lot of TV programs and computer games are violent and destructive. A report by the Australian Early

Childhood Foundation suggests that by the time they finish primary school, children would have seen over 8,000 murders and 100,000 acts of violence on TV. As a result, violence and bullying increase in the playground as children are conditioned that anti-social behaviour is acceptable. Child psychologists also warn that watching death and violence at an early age can harm children emotionally and psychologically.

Parents should also be hard headed about at what age their children get a mobile phone and join social networking groups like Facebook and YouTube. Mobile phones are not only expensive and take time away from interacting with friends face to face, they can also be used for cyber bullying. While playground bullying has been around for years, and is more obvious and easier to deal with, cyber bullying often happens without parents or teachers knowing about it. Given the technology, cyber bullying can also be like an infection that spreads quickly across the mobile network or internet and that the victim is powerless to deal with or control.

New technologies – unhealthy

Time spent in front of TV and on computers and the internet means time not spent on other healthier activities. Australia, and other Western societies, are facing an obesity crisis with many children no longer physically active. Instead of running around outdoors, riding bikes or taking up sport, children spend most of the time on computers, the internet or watching TV. One US study found that children watch TV for three to four hours a day, ending up with more time in front of the screen than in the classroom over their years at school. An Australian Bureau of Statistics survey involving 2.7 million children discovered that when it came to activities outside school hours, in the two week period of the survey:

- 97% (2.7 million) had watched television, DVDs or videos.
- 83% (2.3 million) had spent time on other screen-based activities.

- 82% (2.2 million) had done homework or other study.
- 72% (2.0 million) had read for pleasure.
- 60% (1.6 million) had been bike riding.
- 49% (1.3 million) had been skateboarding, rollerblading or riding a scooter.
- 48% (1.3 million) had spent time on art and craft activities.

No wonder many children are overweight and lack physical coordination and strength. There are also the problems of children missing out on the pleasure of being creative by ignoring art and craft and failing to learn how team sports can teach the benefits of cooperation and supporting others.

What should parents do?

There is no doubt that technology is a daily part of our lives and that it brings many benefits. At the same time, there are harmful consequences. Children have a very versatile, powerful and cheap computer with them all day, every day – it sits on their shoulders and it's called a brain. Make sure they use it! Parents should:

- in the first five to six years, keep children away from Game-Boys, computers and TV and concentrate on reading, playing educational games, being physically active, listening to music, and interacting with other children and adults;
- supervise what children watch on TV and how they use computers and the internet and make sure it is appropriate;
- monitor their children's behaviour, especially for signs that playing games, surfing the net or using social sites is becoming compulsive or addictive;
- ban TVs and computers from bedrooms and also during meal times; AND
- when choosing a school make sure you find out about how the new technologies are being used and if there is a balance between traditional styles of teaching and one where computers, electronic whiteboards and e-books dominate.

3

Ground Helicopter Parents & Let Children Take Risks

It's only natural that parents love their children, are concerned about their safety and do everything they can to make sure they are protected. But, there is a danger of being over-protective and keeping your children so close that they never learn to be independent and able to deal with life's challenges.

Helicopter parents take to the air

Think trampolines. Walk around your neighbourhood or visit friends with children and if you see a trampoline, it's guaranteed that there will be a safety net cocooning children and making sure they don't fall off. How did children cope for all those years without a safety net? While no parent wants a child with a sprained ankle or injured arm, the reality is that taking risks, being aware of danger and, on the odd occasion, getting hurt are all part of growing up and developing resilience.

For me, growing up in Broadmeadows, a working class suburb north of Melbourne, during the 1960s was the best of times. As children, our parents gave us the freedom to ride bikes all day, swim in the local creek, climb trees, make cubby houses and play football and cricket out on the street. The only time we went home was to sleep, to eat and to do our homework. Today's children are the opposite. Most of their time is spent in-doors, on the internet, playing computer games or watching TV and DVDs.

As a child at Campmeadows Primary School I also, along with other kids, had the freedom to play dodge ball and British bulldog during recess and lunchtime – games that many schools have now banned.

Today's parents are fearful about their children's safety and keep them cocooned in a safe environment.

A 2007 survey of UK children carried out by *Play England* found that:

- over 50% of 7 to 12 year olds were not allowed to climb trees,
- 21% said that they had been banned from playing conkers, and
- 17% were stopped from playing chasey.

Another UK report, *Risk and Childhood*, by the Royal Society of the Arts, found that while in 1971, 80% of years seven to eight children travelled to school on their own, by 1990 the figure had dropped to just 9%.

In the US they are called helicopter parents and they're easy to recognise. Always hovering around, wrapping their children in cotton wool and never letting them take risks, do anything dangerous or give them the freedom to do what children normally love doing the most – getting away from parents and doing their own thing. The US author Lenore Skenazy created a furore and was attacked as America's worst mum when she allowed her nine year old son to travel on the New York subway by himself. Skenazy argues that modern parents smother their children with too much attention and, as a result, children are always in the safety zone and never learn to take risks and be adventurous.

As argued by the Western Australian researcher Dr. Lisa Wood, the co-author of a report by the Victorian Health Promotion Foundation, called *Nothing but fear itself*, "The negative impacts of parental fear and resulting 'cotton wool' kids are increasingly being recognised as having adverse impacts on children, including less healthy lifestyles and increasing obesity levels ... Children are also missing out on opportunities to develop important life skills that can be learnt through independent play and being allowed to move around within their neighbourhoods".

Helicopter parents can also try too hard with their child's schooling, always up at the school asking questions, chasing teachers to get what they think will be the best for their child and interfering with what is being taught. While it's OK for parents to take an interest in their child's education, there is a fine line between being genuinely concerned and turning into somebody who ends up nagging teachers and interfering.

It's not just parents guilty of wrapping their children in cotton wool, the movement in schools to teach self-esteem and to make sure every child is a winner by banning red pens and no longer failing children also contributes to children who dislike criticism and who always expect to be praised. As noted by a UK child behaviour expert, Dr. Carol Craig, an obsession with promoting self-esteem has led to a narcissistic generation where children feel they are beyond criticism and that they can do no wrong.

Australian schools have also been criticised for banning children doing cartwheels in the playground and there are so many regulations and legal requirements surrounding school camps that many teachers have given up on organising outdoor adventure activities.

Advertising and the commercialisation of childhood are also to blame for creating generations of children who are forced to grow up too quickly and are denied the challenges and risks associated with running free. Every day, children are bombarded with advertising to buy the last technological gadget, to mimic celebrity fashions and lifestyles and to outspend their friends with whatever is the trend of the day. No wonder that a British inquiry into childhood, commissioned by The Children's Society, recommended a ban on advertising for children under 12 and that, within Australia, there is a move to ban junk food advertising during children's TV programs.

Helicopter parents – what do they look like?

Helicopter parents start wrapping their children in cotton wool at a very early age. Whether it's using a breathing monitor to check the new born infant when he or she is asleep or setting up a video monitor to make sure you can watch what they are doing 24/7 when you are in another room, it's obvious that today's parents are very different from previous generations.

While keeping a watchful eye is important, gone are the days when as long as babies were dry, fed and not in distress that parents left them alone, trusted that things were OK and got on with their own lives. Dressing babies is also now a million dollar business with parents outdoing one another with the latest fashions from stores like Pumpkin Patch and Seed. Gen-Y parents, maybe because they have children late in life and have only one or two, are especially guilty of pampering and praising their children and making them feel they should always be the centre of attention.

Children once walked or rode their bikes to school – not any more. In cities and suburbs around Australia there are fleets of 4-wheel drives and SUVs lining up every day to drop off and pick up children when they are at school. Helicopter parents are also the first to take sides with their children whenever an incident occurs at school or a teacher raises a complaint. With mobile phones the situation is getting out of control and it's not unusual for students, after being punished by a teacher, to immediately phone or SMS their parents and complain about how they have been treated and to try and get them on side.

Now that education departments across Australia are putting teachers, students and parents in instant contact with one another via the internet, with every child and their teacher being identified, expect the situation to get worse, especially for teachers who are now on call every day of the week whenever they log on and check their email. Once upon a time, except for correcting some work and preparing for the next day, when teachers left after a long, tiring day at school they could go home and relax and recharge – not any more.

The old adage about children 'being seen but not heard' is obviously a saying that helicopter parents have never heard of judged by the way their children talk incessantly, interrupt others and demand to be heard. Hear them at the local supermarket complaining about not getting what they want, on the train, tram or bus telling their parents where they should go for their holidays or at family gatherings interrupting others and refusing to sit quietly and listen or to go outside to play.

Helicopter parents turn ugly

The majority of parents are thoughtful, patient and balanced when it comes to their children and dealing with others, not like those helicopter parents suffering from an angry parent syndrome when dealing with teachers. Increasingly, teachers are being threatened with violence and abuse from toxic parents and the situation at some schools is so bad that more and more teachers are taking stress leave or leave the profession altogether. In Victoria the number of stress related WorkCover claims is on the increase, and the head of the Victorian Australian Education Union, Mary Bluett, claims that the reason is, "You've got the angry parent syndrome, where they come into the classroom and abuse the teacher in front of the class … That sort of behaviour, where someone is at work and stressed in the first place – it becomes a trigger that tips them over".

Parents can also turn ugly when watching their children play sport. So many parents are abusing umpires, swearing at the opposition and haranguing their children that the Australian Sports Commission has established a website to deal with the problem. On its website, the Commission warns that, "While some junior players this winter may catch the flu – some spectators are likely to be struck down by a much more dangerous affliction – 'ugly parents' syndrome!".

Why do we have helicopter parents?

Read the daily paper, watch the evening news or listen to the radio and it's understandable why parents worry about their children's safety.

The world out there is a dangerous place and every day there are examples of street violence, homes being broken into, robbery, sexual attacks and children being threatened. Take the example of Victoria, with newspaper headlines like "Crime creeps into every corner of Victoria", "Violent crime up in Victoria" and "Eastern Victoria is crime ridden" it's no wonder that parents are concerned for their children's safety.

But, has crime grown worse and are children more at risk? Again, using the example of Victoria, and based on the statistics gathered by the Victorian Police, it's clear that overall rates have gone down over time, instead of getting worse. In 2009/2010 there was a decline in the crime rate of 6.4% per 100,000 people and, when comparing the period between 2000/2001 and 2009/2010, the crime rate decreased by 29.9%. For the same period the number of recorded offences decreased by 19.3%. While schools are being made to teach children about "stranger danger", Victorian research suggests that parents' fears are exaggerated. In the report, *Nothing but fear itself*, the statement is made that, "There is no evidence to indicate any fundamental change over time of threats to children by actual crimes of abduction, robbery, assault and homicide committed against them by strangers".

One of the unintended consequences of China's one child policy is a generation of children labelled "little emperors". It stands to reason, when parents have only one child to raise, instead of 3, 4 or 5, that the child would get undivided attention and parents place all their hopes and expectations on the one chance they will have to raise a boy or girl. While there are no restrictions on the number of children Western parents can have, it's no secret that countries like Australia and England face declining birth rates and families are having fewer children. Modern parents, compared to parents during the '50s and '60s, tend to lavish more care and attention on their children and are less willing to give them the freedom they need to takes risks and be independent.

Why helicopter parents need to be grounded

We all have to grow up and learn to be adults but, children need to be children first. Wrapping children in cotton wool denies them the fun and excitement of childhood. Keeping them cocooned also stops them from learning the skills they need to be independent, to take risks and to develop resilience and the ability to overcome challenges and adversity.

The most obvious problem with stopping children being involved in physical activities and games and allowing them to spend hours and hours in-doors is that they become unfit and overweight. Western societies are suffering an obesity crisis due to junk food and our sedentary lifestyle and children are especially at risk. In Australia, based on figures gathered as part of the 2007/2008 National Health Survey, 24.9% of children between 5-17 years of age are overweight or obese.

The first stage in teaching a child to ride a bike usually involves trainer wheels – but, at some stage the trainer wheels have to be taken off and your child needs to ride alone. The odd scratch, bruise or sprained wrist are inevitable and a vital part of becoming an accomplished rider. As children master something physically challenging, like riding a bike, climbing a tree or swimming across a creek, in addition to keeping healthy and fit, they develop confidence in their ability to do something difficult. As the saying, 'if at first you don't succeed, try, try again' suggests, children also need to learn that perseverance is important and that some of the most rewarding things in life don't happen easily or at first attempt; they take effort and application.

Children also need to socialise and interact with others their own age, without adults interfering or acting as guardians ready to intervene at the slightest hint of trouble. Children can be rough on one another and bullying does sometimes happen but, unless matters are serious, children should be left to their own devices to sort things out. By playing games, interacting with others and resolving personality clashes and disagreements children learn vital social skills that will be important in later life.

While it is natural for parents to want to protect their children and stop them from doing anything dangerous, it is also important that children learn to deal with fear and to draw on their own resources, physical and emotional, to conquer risky situations. Activities like adventure camps or joining groups like the School Cadets or the Scouts allow children to push themselves physically, to overcome their fears and to experience the satisfaction of achieving something difficult.

4
Back to Basics

The Three R's (reading, writing and arithmetic) are the basics, especially during the primary school years, and for most parents they are central to their child's education.

What ever happened to the basics?

By the time they leave primary school, if children cannot read and write correctly, if they are unable to recite their times tables, do mental arithmetic and basic addition, subtraction, multiplication and division then they will have little chance of succeeding in secondary school.

The sad reality is that once children fall behind they rarely, if ever, catch up and achieve as well as their classmates. One of the strongest indicators of whether a student will do well at Year 12 is how well he or she has performed lower down in the school – making it essential that schools teach the basics and teach them well.

The problem is that many schools in England, Australia and the US no longer teach the basics properly and, as a result, standards have failed to improve and many children leave primary school destined for failure. The situation is so bad that many parents employ tutors to get their children up to speed or enrol them in out of school programs like Kumon to strengthen English and mathematics skills.

In schools, calculators have taken over and children rely on them so much that they are incapable of mental arithmetic – just watch teenagers paying for something at the supermarket and, if they don't have a calculator, trying to work out how much change they should get!

Some teachers argue that children do not have to be taught how to spell or memorise difficult words as computers have a spell check.

In many classrooms teachers argue that children learning to read is as easy and natural as learning to talk and that reading does not have to be taught the old-fashioned way using phonics and phonemic awareness.

When it comes to writing essays, some teachers also argue that students do not have to be taught grammar, punctuation and syntax (how sentences are structured) as the rules of English can be picked up as you go along or when you need them.

Instead of learning times tables by heart or memorising poems and historical dates, learning by rote is described as "drill and kill" and attacked for making learning boring and mechanical. Trendy teachers argue that if students need to find out something, all they need to do is to go on the internet and search for what they want. Some years ago the then Western Australian Minister for Education even went as far as arguing that teachers are obsolete as computers and the internet can teach students all they need to know.

Instead of direct instruction where teachers decide and manage what is being taught, progressive teachers also argue that students need to take control of their own learning and have the freedom to decide what they do in the classroom. While freedom is important, parents and teachers need to understand the difference between 'freedom from' and 'freedom to'. Being free to achieve something difficult (like playing the clarinet or analysing a poem) requires hard work, application and being taught. While being free to do your own thing (like studying whatever topic you want) might look attractive and enjoyable, if you have not been taught how to master something complex and difficult then such learning rarely happens by accident. If children only did what they wanted when at school then learning would be superficial and narrow, as teachers generally know more than their students. Instead of giving the classroom over to students, it is the teacher's job to introduce children to the knowledge and skills that will challenge, enrich and enlarge their understanding of the world.

The reading wars

It's called the reading wars and it's a battle that has spread across Australia, New Zealand, the US and the UK. On one side are those arguing that the best way to teach children to read is whole language and on the other side are those arguing for what is called a phonics and phonemic awareness approach. The battle has led to parliamentary inquiries across the English-speaking world and fierce debates between academics and teachers. The reading wars have also been fuelled by worries that standards have fallen over the years because of the introduction of whole language and because unacceptable numbers of children continue to leave primary school and go into secondary school unable to properly read and write. In Australia, a 1996 national literacy test showed that 27% of year 3 children and 30% of year 5 children were below the standard required for successful learning.

Phonics and phonemic awareness

Phonics and phonemic awareness is a way of teaching reading that stresses the importance of beginning readers learning the relationship between letters and groups of letters and sounds. Each letter in the alphabet is represented by a particular sound, for example, the letter 'b' is represented by the sound 'buh' and words can be divided into phonemes (the smallest unit), for example 'dog' has three phonemes 'd/o/g'. Children need to be taught the rules of reading in a structured and systematic way, including being able to identify vowels and consonants and those words in the English language that prove the exception to the rule.

Whole language

With a whole language approach, instead of children being formally taught the relationship between letters and groups of letters and sounds in an isolated way, are expected to recognise words by their context. When learning to read the focus is on meaning and children are asked to "look and guess" by working out what a word is by its place in the story or what is suggested by the accompanying illustration or cartoon. Whole language is based on the mistaken belief that in the same way children learned to speak naturally, so too can they learn to read without any direct instruction based on phonics. While it is true that many children pick up reading without much effort there are many others, especially boys, who need to be taught according to a phonics and phonemic awareness approach. Parents need to understand that one of the main reasons boys misbehave and get into trouble in the classroom is because they have not been taught to read properly.

Fuzzy maths

In the same way that teaching reading has changed over the years, mathematics has also been transformed – as shown by the following tongue-in-cheek description circulating on the internet.

- **Teaching Math in 1950:** A logger sells a truckload of lumber for $100. His cost of production is 4/5 of the price. What is his profit?

- **Teaching Math in 1960:** A logger sells a truckload of lumber for $100. His cost of production is 4/5 of the price, or $80. What is his profit?

- **Teaching Math in 1970:** A logger exchanges a set "L" of lumber for a set "M" of money. The cardinality of set "M" is 100. Each element is worth one dollar. Make 100 dots representing the elements of the set "M". The set "C", the cost of production contains 20 fewer points than set "M." Represent the set "C" as a subset of set "M" and answer the following question: What is the cardinality of the set "P" for Profits?

- **Teaching Math in 1980:** A logger sells a truckload of lumber for $100. Her cost of production is $80 and her profit is $20. Your assignment: Underline the number 20.
- **Teaching Math in 1990:** By cutting down beautiful forest trees, the logger makes $20. What do you think of this way of making a living? Topic for class participation after answering the question: How did the forest birds and squirrels feel as the logger cut down the trees? There are no wrong answers.

In the US the more recent approach to teaching mathematics is called 'fuzzy maths' and, instead of memorising times tables, mental arithmetic, learning by rote and mastering basic algorithms like long division, students use calculators, work in open classrooms, manage their own learning and are expected to relate mathematics to 'real-world' applications. Instead of arriving at the correct answer, children are congratulated for going through the right process and they spend a lot of time working in groups.

Rote learning and memorisation are good

When it comes to learning by rote one the advantages is that the approach fits in with how young children best learn. While play, being creative and discovery learning are also necessary, it is vital that children first develop and strengthen their ability to memorise and automatically recall facts, numbers, dates and events. Take the example of times tables and learning them off by heart. If children do not know their times tables they will find it difficult to solve mathematical problems. In the words of the US educationalist E.D. Hirsch, "… varied and repeated practice leading to rapid recall and automaticity is necessary to higher-order problem-solving skills in both mathematics and science". The human brain can only deal with and process so much at any one time and when trying to solve a problem, if all a child's brain power is being used to get the basics right, then there will be nothing left to solve the problem in front of them.

Reading provides another example of needing to do things automatically and being taught what you need to know so it becomes second nature. If children have never been taught to read properly then as they try to read a paragraph they will be forced to spend time stumbling over every word and trying to guess what the sentence or passage might mean, making it frustrating and difficult to work out what the author wants to convey. Playing a musical instrument is the same, months and sometimes years have to be spent practising and repeating scales before being able to play a difficult and extended piece.

Why direct instruction is important

While there are many different approaches to teaching and good teachers use a range of strategies, depending on the subject and what students are expected to learn, research shows that memorisation and rote learning are very important, especially when it comes to teaching the basics during the primary school years. Research in America comparing different teaching styles and strategies (called *Project Follow Through*) also concludes that direct instruction is the more effective. It makes sense that it is far easier for a teacher to manage and monitor a class of 25 as a group instead of trying to individually deal with every child on a one to one basis. John Sweller, an academic at the University of New South Wales, also argues that it is more effective if teachers teach in a formal, direct way instead of being facilitators and letting children discover their own learning. After examining the different approaches to teaching over the last 50 years Sweller concludes, "… information should always be presented in direct rather than indirect form … This principle applies equally to all educational contexts but flies in the face of much educational theory of the last few decades". One of the reasons many teachers burn out and leave the profession is because of the pressure to provide an individualised learning plan and to monitor, assess and evaluate every individual child.

Why too much testing is bad

Such have been the fears about falling standards and concerns about whole language and fuzzy maths that governments across the English-speaking world have introduced national testing in literacy and numeracy at the various levels of schooling. In Australia there is testing at years 3, 5, 7 and 9 every year and the results comparing schools are placed on the *My School* website. Parents can get details about schools they might want to send their children to and after the results are released there are league tables published ranking schools from best to worst.

While schools should be held accountable and parents deserve information about how schools are performing, based on what has happened in England and the US, especially New York, there are dangers in too much testing and using the results to name and shame schools. The dangers include:

- teachers being so worried about test results that they focus so much on the basics that the curriculum is narrowed and children miss out on subjects like music, physical education, history and literature,
- in order to make sure they get the best results, schools refusing to enrol children they think will under-perform or asking under-performing children to stay at home on the day of the test,
- teachers being pressured to cheat by giving children the right answers, and
- the way the tests are designed and measured, while appearing scientific and objective, being unreliable and invalid. As the saying goes, 'there are lies, damned lies and statistics'.

When choosing a school for your child, while it is important to find out how well the school performs in tests and examinations, it is also important to know that the school is not a test factory, that students are taught a rich and balanced curriculum and that the school values those aspects of education that are not so easily measured.

5
Children need a Moral Compass

Listen to the news, read the paper, watch TV, travel on public transport or walk through a shopping arcade and it's easy to see why many argue that young people have the lost the plot when it comes to knowing the difference between right and wrong and how they should behave.

A world without a moral compass

Being civil and polite to others seems to have gone the way of black and white TVs and vinyl records! When is the last time you saw a young person (or even an adult) offer his or her seat to someone more needy in a tram or a train? How many times have you had the experience of being knocked or pushed aside as somebody rushes through the doorway at a cinema or restaurant? Even family get-togethers are not immune as children expect to be the centre of attention and to get what they want when they want it.

Police talk about young people's lack of respect for authority and how selfish and violent behaviour leads to blood on the streets. Teachers complain about classes where children are rude and disruptive and where they refuse to consider others. Simple things like not putting your feet on a train seat, not shouting into your mobile phone when in a restaurant and looking directly at someone when you are talking to them appear to have been lost. The situation is so bad that the Australian Government, during the time John Howard was Prime Minister, made every school across Australia teach values education. Millions of dollars were spent on classroom resources, teacher training and workshops and conferences teaching students about values that were once taught in the home and by parents, such as *respect, responsibility, fair go, care and compassion and understanding, tolerance and inclusion*. Both Labor and Liberal/National Governments have also supported a *Chaplains in School* program to teach students about morals and ethics and to help them work out what values they need to lead a good life.

Where have we gone wrong?

Why do so many young people lack a moral compass and appear to put self-interest before considering others? The English writer, Lynne Truss, in her book *Talking to the Hand* argues that modern society is to blame. The way we live is so busy and rushed, advertising and our consumer society are all based on the idea, "if it feels good, do it" and we now have a celebrity culture where having affairs, taking drugs and spending millions on 'life-style' is the norm. The fact that religious beliefs are not as strong as they once were and fewer children now go to Sunday school or to church also helps to explain why so many young people know little about morality and the best way to behave. No wonder that a survey of students at England's Durham University found that only 1 in 20 could name the 10 Commandments and that most thought the Bible was old-fashioned. Finally, home entertainment centres, computer games, the internet, mobile phones and social networking sites are also to blame. While the new technologies have some positives, spending hours playing computer games (especially those that are violent and destructive) de-sensitises children and teaches them that violence is acceptable. Hours and hours on social networking sites, instead of meeting friends face to face, leads to young people forgetting how to interact and to deal with others.

What's to be done?

The first thing parents need to realise is that education, especially moral education, begins in the home and that equally as important as feeding, clothing and giving a child love and affection is the need to teach them how to behave and what constitutes good and bad behaviour. Babies might be born with certain physical characteristics, dark or blond hair, blue or green eyes and a predisposition to certain illnesses like high blood pressure but, they are not born with a moral compass. Children do not simply wake up one day knowing the difference between right and wrong and what is a fair and just way to treat themselves and others.

Parents have a vital role to play as they are responsible for teaching their children the importance of ethical values and ways of thinking, feeling and acting that lead to being responsible and civil. Such characteristics include:

- realising that there is more to life than self-interest and simply getting what you want, when you want it,
- accepting that along with rights come responsibilities,
- understanding others' interests and needs and caring about their feelings and wants,
- considering the consequences of one's thoughts and actions and realising that whatever one does will impact on oneself and others, and
- being aware of one's own needs, ethical, physical and emotional and developing a moral code by which to live.

For many parents, it is their religion that offers a moral code by which to live and to raise their children. The great religions of the world (including Christianity, Judaism, Islam, Buddhism and Hinduism) provide morals and ethics that guide one's actions and teach what is the best way to live. For religious non-believers there are also the types of values and beliefs associated with living in a just and democratic society, one where the guiding principle is to achieve the greatest happiness for the greatest number of people. Secular societies like Australia and the United States, while owing a great debt to Christianity, work on the assumption that we should be guided by values like tolerance, compassion, civility, being honest and telling the truth, respecting human dignity and not doing harm to oneself and to others.

Developing a moral compass

Parents need to understand that if they do not provide a clear and consistent ethical and moral framework in which their children can grow then it will happen by default – often, with bad results. When viewing TV or watching movies, surfing the internet, playing computer games or simply watching others in the home, at school or in the playground, children are learning about behaviour.

As briefly mentioned in Chapter 1, one way to introduce children to the types of positive and life-affirming values that are so necessary for a civilised society is by introducing them to traditional and modern sayings, fairy tales, myths, legends and stories. Stories and lessons from the Bible and other sacred texts from the world's great religions are also vitally important in helping children develop a strong moral compass.

Even for non-Christians, the Bible offers a significant reservoir of lessons and proverbs that, while hundreds of years old, are still relevant to today's society. The story of the *Good Samaritan* tells children about the importance of being charitable and helping others. Jesus' command, "let he who without sin cast the first stone", suggests that it is wrong to condemn or punish others without first looking at oneself and understanding that each one of us is far from perfect. The 10 Commandments offer a clear and succinct moral code by which to live and commandments like "do not steal", "love your neighbour as yourself", "do not commit murder" and "honour your father and your mother" provide the foundation for a peaceful and rewarding way of life.

Aphorisms like "many hands make light work", "never put off till tomorrow, what you can do today" and "a poor workman blames his tools" help young children to understand important lessons about life and, hopefully, to better prepare them for the challenges ahead. Children's stories like those in *Aesop's Fables* such as *The Tortoise and the Hare*, *The Boy Who Cried Wolf* and *The Ant and the Grasshopper* have the strength of conveying important moral lessons in a simple and direct way that young children enjoy listening to and that also have the benefit of exciting their imagination. Take *The Ant and the Grasshopper* – like the grasshopper, young children very much live in the here and now, expect that their needs will be met sooner rather than later and that others will always provide for them. When winter strikes the grasshopper, who had spent his time enjoying himself over summer, is left with nothing to eat, while the industrious and forward-looking ants have enough supplies to live on until the next spring.

Ancient myths and legends like *Pandora's Box*, *Narcissus*, *Icarus*, *The Iliad* and *The Odyssey* also provide a rich resource that introduces children to significant values and beliefs, while not often immediately relevant and useful, that provide valuable lessons that will help and guide them in later life. Narcissus is so consumed by his own beauty that, on seeing his reflection in a pond, falls in love with his own image and withers away. Icarus falls to his death after ignoring his father's warning about flying too close to the sun. Narcissus warns of the danger of idolising oneself (or being narcissistic) and Icarus of the consequences of being overly ambitious and refusing to recognise one's limitations.

Of course, different cultures and different religions will have their own legends, stories and moral teachings and there is much to learn and value in what they offer. The African proverb, "It takes a village" tells us that while parents are central to a child's upbringing, the wider community, including neighbours, friends, extended family and institutions like schools and the church, also have an important role to play. The Chinese story, the *Fifteen Honest Coins*, tells of a young boy who finds a bag of money in a market place and, after being advised by his mother, looks for the owner of the lost money. The boy's honesty and the attempts by a merchant to unfairly claim it as his, leads to a judge's decision to give the 15 coins to the boy.

The saying, from the Buddhist sacred text the *Dhammapada*, "He who does not rouse himself when it is time to rise, who, though young and strong is full of sloth, whose will and thought are weak, that lazy and idle man never finds the way to knowledge" is something all children would benefit from learning. The Taoist aphorism attributed to Lao-tzu, "He who is naturally in sympathy with man, to him all men come. But he who forcedly adapts, has no room for himself, still less for others. And he who has no room for others, has no ties. It is all over for him", tells of an important human truth that is constant across many cultures and religions.

Don't feed children pap

At the same time as writing this chapter a debate erupted in Victoria about some schools giving children a book to read that dealt with violence, suicide and murder. The assumption is that the best way to grab children's attention is to give them books that deal with the dark side of human nature. Video games like *Grand Theft Auto* work on the same assumption – one where the belief is that children enjoy violence, blowing things up and killing people. A related approach to children's reading, especially for boys, involves books like *The Day My Bum Went Psycho* and *Zombie Bums from Uranus*. By writing about bums, vomit, farting and crude jokes, the belief is that such books will be immediately entertaining and popular and that it doesn't matter what children read (especially boys), as long as they are reading.

Wrong. Violent video games and crude and offensive books are morally empty and designed to appeal to the base side of human nature. While films like *Star Wars* and books like *The Lion, the Witch and the Wardrobe* also deal with death and violence, such texts also have much to say about right and wrong and about morality. C.S. Lewis was a Christian and his Narnia books have a strong religious element to them. Following the children's journey after entering Narnia, it's clear that many of the challenges and difficulties they face have a strong moral element. Emotions like jealousy, betrayal, bravery, forgiveness and selflessness are all experienced as the battle between good and evil ebbs and flows. Similarly, with the "Star Wars" films there is a battle between the dark and the good side of the force. The violence and destruction we see in the film is not simply there for it's own sake, but to show the inhumane and life-denying consequences of succumbing to the dark side of the force and the need to remain true to the better side of one's nature.

6
Cultural Literacy: What All Children Should Know

Read the newspapers, listen to the radio, watch TV and surf the net and you will soon learn the importance of cultural literacy. Every day we come across situations where somebody refers to a historical event or scientific fact, quotes from literature or uses a saying to make a point and, unless you know what is being referred to, you are in the dark.

And if you are in the dark – what about your children?

Sayings like "too many cooks spoil the broth" and "a stitch in time saves nine".

References from the past, like "he met his Waterloo", "it's his Achilles' heel", "she opened a Pandora's box" and "it's beyond the pale".

Political and legal references, like "separation of powers", "hung parliament", "executive government", "a Westminster parliamentary system", "habeas corpus" and "innocent until proven guilty".

Literary sayings, like "the horror, the horror", "to err is human, to forgive divine" and "the past is a foreign country, they do things differently there".

References and sayings from the Bible, like "pride cometh before a fall" and "an eye for an eye, a tooth for a tooth".

Scientific references, like global warming, IVF and AIDS.

TV quiz shows like *Who Wants to be a Millionaire?* are also big on cultural literacy, as are crosswords and games like scrabble.

Understanding the news, following public debates and doing well at trivia nights are not the only reasons why it is important to make sure that your children are culturally literate.

Why cultural literacy is important – citizenship

Countries like England, the US, Australia and New Zealand are democracies that owe their freedom, stability and peaceful way of life to a system of government and legal institutions that are unique. If liberal democracies like ours are to survive and prosper then it is vital that each generation is taught how our system works, its origins and how it has evolved and their rights and responsibilities as future citizens. Teaching civics and citizenship, in subjects like history and social studies, should be a central part of any school curriculum and children must be taught the core values and beliefs that safeguard our way of life. While not all countries have compulsory voting, as Australia does, it is important for a healthy and robust society that citizens are knowledgeable about politics and that they vote in an informed way. Each one of us also needs to be aware of our legal rights and responsibilities as well as being able to recognise corruption and waste in government and when politicians seek to gain too much power.

Why cultural literacy is important – national identity

Each nation and various ethnic and religious groups have their own history and special way of life and it is important to accept and tolerate difference and diversity. At the same time, to safeguard social stability and cohesion there must be support for the institutions, values and beliefs that form the common ground on which communities are built and that bind them. In a speech titled "The Genius of Australian Multiculturalism" (given at the Sydney Institute in February, 2011) the Commonwealth Government's Minister for Immigration and Citizenship, Chris Bowen, argued that while it is good to celebrate different cultures and beliefs, that migrants wanting to settle in

Australia should respect Australian values. The Minister said:

> Firstly, our multiculturalism is underpinned by respect for traditional Australian values. Those who arrive in Australia are invited to continue to celebrate their cultures and traditions, not only within a broader culture of freedom but, more importantly, with respect.
>
> However, if there is any inconsistency between these cultural values and the values of individual freedom and the rule of law, then these traditional Australian values win out. They must. This has been the case since multiculturalism was introduced as Australian policy in the 1970s.

While it's true that we live in a global village and many Western societies are multicultural it is also important that children understand and appreciate what is distinctive about the culture of the country in which they live. Australia is a Western liberal democracy and many of the nation's institutions, values and beliefs can be traced to our Judeo-Christian heritage. While it's true, geographically, that Australia is part of Asia, it's also true that our culture is unique and, as anybody who has travelled overseas will know, our way of life is very different from places like Indonesia, Thailand, Vietnam and Cambodia.

Children knowing about cultural literacy and civics and citizenship do not happen by accident; they have to be taught.

Popular culture not enough

It's also the case that while children learn a good deal from TV, the internet, their friends and popular culture, it is only at school that there is an opportunity to study important subjects like history and literature in a systematic, balanced and thoughtful way. It's also important to acknowledge that cultural literacy deals with those events, dates, people, movements, art works and literature that have something significant to say about our culture and that stand the test of time. The reason Shakespeare's plays and Jane Austen's novels will always be popular, unlike the latest Mills and Boon romance or a Van

Damme action movie, is that they deal with human emotions and relationships in a very moving, dramatic and compelling way.

Schools are important

While parents have a crucial role to play in helping their children become culturally literate by introducing them to stories when they are young, taking them to museums and art galleries and introducing them to classical music, it is at school that children have the best chance of learning what they need to know to be well-educated and effective citizens. Schools have a responsibility to teach subjects like history, literature, music, art, social studies, mathematics and science in a detailed and balanced way, making sure that every child is introduced and becomes familiar with what is most important and influential.

The 1960s cultural revolution

Unfortunately, schools no longer teach cultural literacy as they once did. During the late '60s and early '70s many schools got rid of:

- syllabuses (or road maps) detailing what had to be taught at each year level,
- tests and examinations employed to find out how much students knew, and
- inspectors who visited classrooms to make sure teachers were teaching the syllabus.

At the same time many teachers argued that children should be given the freedom to learn what *they* wanted to learn and that teaching subjects like history, literature and science didn't matter as long as students enjoyed themselves.

Many schools, instead of teaching history and making sure children learned about important historical facts, dates, events and people, made children study topics like the local community and what was in the daily news. Instead of being introduced to traditional myths, legends and fables and reading classic literature many teachers believed that children should study popular culture, represented by BMX magazines, comics, TV shows and pop songs.

Testing times

During the '80s and '90s there was a reaction against schools not having syllabuses and regular tests and the fact that many students left schools culturally illiterate. Parents and politicians became concerned that the curriculum had been dumbed down, that standards had fallen, especially with the Three R's, and that many students went on to university or work without the necessary knowledge and skills.

As a result, in countries like England, the US and Australia, governments and education departments reintroduced syllabuses and testing. Once again, though, many students failed to become culturally literate as the syllabuses given to schools lacked detail and solid content. Instead of presenting subjects in a traditional way, the syllabuses focused on what are called skills and competencies, like working in teams, learning how to learn, solving problems and collecting and organising information.

The new syllabuses written during the 80s and 90s were also politically correct. History, for example, was called Studies of Society and the Environment and the focus was on teaching about the dangers of environmental destruction, how women and migrants are oppressed and how Western, capitalist societies are characterised by disadvantage and injustice. In English, instead of studying classic literature like Greek tragedies, Shakespeare and Dickens' novels, students are asked to analyse what are called multi-modal texts (texts that incorporate visual and well as print), SMS messages, film posters and even graffiti. Instead of enjoying literature for what it tells us about human nature and morality, students are made to analyse the way literature teaches prejudice and denies the rights of what are called victim-groups.

The result? Young children are told not to read *Cinderella* as a happy ending is defined as marrying the prince, *Little Black Sambo* is banned as it is offensive to dark skinned people and Enid Blyton's series *The Magic Faraway Tree* is criticised for failing to present girls as physically strong and active. In a school in Victoria a teacher was so worried about political correctness that when his class sang *Kookaburra sits on the old gum tree* he changed the line "gay your life must be" to "fun your life must be" as he did not want to offend homosexuals.

What does your child need to know to be culturally literate?

How you define cultural literacy will depend on who your parents are, where you were born and the type of community to which you belong. The education a Hindu child would receive living by the banks of the Ganges is very different to an Anglo-Celtic child living in Sydney or Melbourne. In the same way, those who are Christian, Muslim or Buddhist will have a different view of the world and the values and beliefs they want to pass on to their children will, generally speaking, be different.

At the same time, if you are part of a Western culture and live in a liberal democracy like Australia or the US, it is possible to identify what your child will need to know to be culturally literate. It's also true that with subjects like mathematics and science, regardless of the culture you live in, there are facts and explanations of the physical world that are common to all.

The following list relates to Australia and should be seen as a starting point. It is not an attempt to cover the entire curriculum that schools should teach, rather it is an outline of the minimum knowledge and understanding required if students are to be knowledgeable and effective members of society.

By the end of compulsory schooling a student should know about:
- A broad outline of Australia's history, geography and culture, both before and after European settlement, and including significant dates, events, people, social and political movements,

geographical, political and economic features and Australia's place in the Asia/Pacific region and the world in general.
- A broad outline of the history of the world, covering prehistoric times until today and including geographic features and evolution as well as the rise and fall of civilisations and different cultures with an emphasis on Western civilisation. Topics should include ancient civilisations such as Sumer and Egypt, early Greece and Rome, Europe and the UK during the Dark and Middle Ages and significant historical periods like the Renaissance, Reformation, Enlightenment and Modern era. While the focus should be on England and Europe and the rise and influence of Christianity, students should also know about other major religions and cultures.
- The music, art and literature central to Western civilisation and Australian culture. Students should know about the fables, myths and legends of early times and the novels, poems and plays that are a central part of the Western literary tradition and also those that are unique to Australia. Art from ancient Greece and Rome and the various periods including the Medieval, Renaissance, Neoclassicism, Romantic, Modern and Contemporary should be covered. Music should emphasise the major works and composers associated with the various movements that have contributed to the evolution of classical music.
- In addition to being studied in their own right, students should know about aspects of mathematics, science and the new technologies they need in order to understand contemporary issues and debates and to cope in an increasingly technological world.

101 things that every child needs to know about Australia

1. Magna Carta
2. Westminster government
3. Separation of powers
4. Habeas Corpus

5. Secret ballot
6. Federation
7. Preferential voting
8. Innocent until proven guilty
9. Common law
10. Communism
11. Totalitarianism
12. Liberal democracy
13. Three levels of government
14. Fascism
15. Popular sovereignty
16. Conciliation and arbitration
17. Globalisation
18. Free trade
19. Protectionism
20. GST
21. Harvester Judgement
22. Right to bargain
23. Capitalism
24. Socialism
25. Compound interest
26. Global warming
27. Climate sceptic
28. Ozone layer
29. El Nino
30. Sustainable development
31. Tropic of Capricorn
32. Carbon reduction
33. Emissions trading scheme
34. Major rivers, including the Snowy, Murray, Murrumbidgee, Yarra, Derwent, Swan, Tamar, Hawkesbury, Yarra and Fitzroy
35. Major mountains, including the Snowy, the Great Dividing Range, Mt Kosciuszko
36. Uluru

37. Great Barrier Reef
38. The Murray/Darling Basin
39. Pilbara
40. North West Shelf
41. Dame Nellie Melba
42. Percy Grainger
43. Dame Edna Everage
44. Important painters, including John Glover, Arthur Streeton, Tom Roberts, Frederick McCubbin, Sidney Nolan, Arthur Boyd, Albert Tucker, Russell Drysdale, John Olsen and Brett Whiteley
45. Waltzing Matilda
46. Back of Bourke
47. Henry Lawson
48. Banjo Paterson
49. The Man from Snowy River
50. David Malouf
51. Patrick White
52. Clancy of the Overflow
53. The Drover's Wife
54. Botany Bay
55. The Getting of Wisdom
56. My Brilliant Career
57. A Fortunate Life
58. My Place
59. David Williamson
60. Judith Wright
61. Kenneth Slessor
62. A.D. Hope
63. Tim Winton
64. John Marsden
65. Sally Morgan
66. The Magic Pudding
67. ANZACS

68. Kokoda Trail
69. Diggers
70. Gallipoli
71. First Fleet
72. Ned Kelly
73. Gold Rushes
74. Eureka Stockade
75. 1788
76. 1901
77. White Australia Policy
78. 1975
79. Western civilisation
80. Christianity
81. Melbourne Cup
82. Phar Lap
83. Evonne Goolagong
84. Cathy Freeman
85. Dawn Fraser
86. Sir Donald Bradman
87. Rod Laver
88. Howard Florey
89. Fred Hollows
90. The Southern Cross
91. The Rocks
92. Sir Gustav Nossal
93. Sir Robert Menzies.
94. Edmund Barton
95. Ben Chifley
96. Riding on the sheep's back
97. Jorn Utzon
98. The lucky country
99. Mary MacKillop
100. Gondwana
101. Neville Bonner

7
How to Choose the Right School

Standing around the BBQ, at dinner with friends or having a chat with neighbours at the local supermarket education is one topic, along with sport and house prices, that is guaranteed to come up.

What are the local schools like? Where are you going to send your children? Are you happy with your child's school? And, if you are lucky enough to have the choice, will it be a Catholic, independent or government school?

As parents understand, no child is ever the same and children, even in the same family, have different abilities, interests and, as they grow older, different ideas about what they want to study, what they want to do after they leave school and the type of career they want to follow.

Choosing the right school for your child is one of the most important and difficult decisions you will have to make. It is also one of the most expensive. Just think of the thousands some parents pay every year in non-government school fees or the cost of buying real estate next to a successful and popular government school to make sure their child is in the school's enrolment zone.

Not all children are the same

It stands to reason, not every child is the same and the reality is that different types of schools will suit different types of children. Even in the early years of growing up, children gravitate to some activities, like reading, enjoying music and playing with shapes and numbers, and not others. Some children have good hand/eye coordination and are quick to learn how to ride their first bike, while others don't really enjoy sport or being physically active.

As children progress through school they begin to develop strengths and weaknesses in certain subjects and activities and likes and dislikes. While some children seem to have a natural ability to learn a language or to play the violin, others are better at playing sport or public speaking and debating. Secondary schools recognise the fact by allowing students to specialise in their final years by choosing between areas of study like the arts, mathematics/science, the humanities, economics/commerce and subjects associated with what is called vocational education and training (VET).

It's also the case that boys and girls, while having a lot in common, have different learning styles and respond in different ways to what happens in the classroom. Girls generally get better results in literacy tests, compared to boys, and boys, compared to girls, need more structure and direction when being told what to do.

It's important that the type of school you choose for your child matches his or her interests and abilities, and fits in with what they want to do after they leave school.

Not all schools are the same

When deciding what type of school will best suit your child it is important to understand that not all schools are the same and that various schools will:

- cater for different types of families and communities,
- have different educational philosophies,
- have different styles of teaching and classroom management,
- have different values and beliefs, and
- have different organisational structures.

Schools can also be divided according to whether they are single sex or co-educational, whether they are selective or open to all and whether they cover all classes from preparatory to year 12 or whether they are a stand alone primary, secondary or senior secondary college.

Various schools will also be managed and controlled in different ways, ranging from government schools that are controlled by state bureaucracies to non-government schools that are managed by a school council or by a particular religious or secular organisation.

Some types of schools are also more successful than others in getting strong results in areas like literacy and numeracy and Year 12 examinations. It is also true that some schools have better resources and facilities than others, are able to attract and keep more effective teachers and offer a richer and broader curriculum and school experience.

Australian schools can be divided into government and non-government. Within government schools there are those that are selective and non-selective and non-government schools can be divided into Catholic and independent. Compared to many overseas countries, Australia has one of the largest non-government school sectors in the world with approximately 34% of students attending such schools, and rising to over 40% at years 11 and 12.

Category	Government	Catholic	Independent
Number of primary schools	4,930	1,225	259
Number of secondary schools	1,040	315	84
Number of full-time teaching staff	162,565	46,807	39,822
Number of full-time students	2,273,915	704,098	483,330

	Government	Catholic	Independent
Total school enrolments expressed as a % (2008)	66%	20.2%	13.8%

Such is the popularity of Catholic and independent schools that over the ten year period 1998-2008 their enrolments grew by 21.9% while government school enrolments flat-lined at 1.1%.

Government schools

Government schools (otherwise known as state or public schools) enrol approximately 66% of Australian students and are managed and controlled by state and territory education departments.

State schools are described as "free, compulsory and secular" and they have a strong tradition of being open to all students and of providing a comprehensive education both at the primary and secondary level. While government schools are controlled by education bureaucracies, teach the same curriculum and have the same employment conditions for teachers, over recent years there has been a move to give schools greater control over how they are managed. State and federal governments have realised that one of the best ways to raise standards and to strengthen government schools is to give them greater freedom in areas like staffing, budgets and curriculum focus.

In Victoria, for example, school councils appoint principals, schools have control over budgets and control over who they employ as teachers.

While technical schools have long since disappeared in Australia with all schools now being made to teach the same curriculum, over recent years there has been a growth in what are called selective secondary schools, especially in Victoria and New South Wales. Selective schools recognise that not all students are the same and such schools have the freedom to concentrate on a particular curriculum area, such as music and the arts, science and technology, or the more traditional, academic curriculum.

Selective secondary schools are very popular with parents, given their very strong Year 12 results and ability to offer a school environment that best meets the abilities and interests of different groups of students. Unlike other government schools, selective schools have entrance examinations and tests and are only open to those students who meet the entry requirements.

While, in theory, government schools are open to all, many, especially the most popular and successful, have entry requirements that families must meet. Requirements include living in the school's enrolment zone, having a brother or sister already in the school, having a parent who attended the school as a student or the student having special needs or abilities that only that school can address.

Government schools that achieve strong Year 12 results are especially popular and, as a result, parents buy houses and property near successful schools to make sure their children will be enrolled. Just witness the number of real estate auctions where houses are advertised on the basis of how close they are to the local much sought after school.

Non-government schools

The non-government sector can be divided into Catholic and independent schools and encompasses a range of faith-based schools including Catholic, Anglican, Presbyterian, Baptist, Jewish and Islamic and secular schools, such as Steiner and Montessori.

Unlike state schools that operate within a government system of education non-government schools are managed at the local level by the school's council, an affiliated religious group or by a church organisation. The overwhelming majority of non-government schools are religious in character and, when compared to government schools, have greater flexibility and freedom to better reflect the needs, aspirations and beliefs of the communities they serve.

As already mentioned, Catholic and independent schools are increasingly popular, even given the thousands needed every year to pay school fees. Surveys of parents suggest that non-government

schools are popular with parents because such schools:
- achieve strong academic results as measured by literacy and numeracy tests, Year 12 examinations and the number of students that go on to tertiary study,
- have a disciplined school environment where students can achieve success in a range of areas, including academic, sporting and co-curricula (debating, public speaking, musicals and school plays),
- have committed teachers and well behaved students, and
- reflect the values that parents see as important, including religious beliefs.

Parents are also attracted by the diverse nature of Catholic and independent schools and the fact, while they have to follow government regulations and requirements in a number of areas, that they have greater control over what and how they teach and how they structure the school environment.

Some non-government schools offer a very traditional approach to education with a focus on academic studies, doing well in tests and examinations and making sure that students are polite, well disciplined and aware of their responsibilities both to one another and to the community in general.

Many non-government schools are also single sex schools, providing an opportunity for girls and boys to be educated separately. While debates rage in the education community about the benefits of single sex and coeducational schools and which is better, it's clear that many parents want the choice.

Seven steps on how to choose the right school for your child
- When it comes to choosing a school remember that children are different and some will prefer and do better in one type of school and not another. Some students are more academic, while others want a more hands on and practical education. Not

all students should go on to tertiary studies, especially when there are alternatives like apprenticeships and doing vocational educational and trade (VET) subjects.
- Talk and listen to neighbours and friends who have their children enrolled in a school that you might be interested in. Nothing beats hearing first hand what families think about the education they have received.
- Australia now has a webpage **www.myschool.edu.au** that lists every government and non-government primary and secondary school in Australia with information about test results and how effective schools are compared to other similar schools. While there are debates about how valid and reliable the information is, the website provides a useful guide to learn more about schools.
- Schools are required to report to their communities on a regular basis and a school's annual report provides a good deal of useful information. Parents can find out about staff qualifications, the school's education program and if it has any special areas or subjects that it concentrates on, where students go after they leave the school and academic results. Some schools also include details about staff morale, parent satisfaction and the number of times students have been suspended or expelled – if they don't publicise the details, you should ask!
- Many schools have open days where parents are invited to walk around the school, watch activities and talk to teachers and staff. While such days are a good way to find out about a school, remember that the day has been carefully planned to present the school in its best light.
- Make a time to visit any school you might be interested in and talk to the principal and staff. While you are there make sure you look at how students are dressed, how they behave and, if you can, observe what is going on in the different classrooms.
- Schools are not all the same and it is important to get answers to a number of key questions, including:

- ➢ what is the school's approach to education – is it progressive or traditional?
- ➢ if it is a primary school, what is the approach to teaching reading, is it whole language or phonics and phonemic awareness?
- ➢ ask how classes are structured, are they mixed ability, open space or the more traditional,
- ➢ what is the school's discipline policy and how does the school deal with badly behaved, disruptive students?
- ➢ what sort of pastoral care program does the school have and how do teachers make sure that students are not being bullied and that they are getting the most out of what the school offers?
- ➢ how extensive is the school's program in areas like sport, music, drama, debating and do all students have a chance to get involved?
- ➢ what is the school's approach to testing and assessment and are classes streamed in terms of ability? A related question is what is the school's policy on supporting gifted students? AND
- ➢ what is the role of computers, the internet and related technologies in the classroom?

8
Coping with Bullying

As parents, we all like to think that our children will be safe at school and that their time in the classroom and the playground will be enjoyable and free from intimidation and violence. Unfortunately, such is not always the case.

A parent's worst nightmare

While not an epidemic, the distressing news is that thousands of Australian school children are victims of bullying and harassment every day. In Victoria, approximately 70 students are suspended every school day and one of the main reasons is because they have bullied others by "threatening behaviour that is a danger to the health, safety and well being". According to Renee Edwards, an academic at the University of South Australia, "around one in four students regularly face overt and covert forms of bullying" and a 2010 survey by Girl Guides Australia involving 24,000 girls aged between 10-14 years found that 68% were concerned about bullying.

The problem is so large that we now have a National Centre Against Bullying **www.ncab.org.au/** and Australia's education ministers, in December 2011, signed up to a National Safe School Framework **www.deewr.gov.au/schooling/nationalsafeschools/Pages/overview.aspx**, including advice to parents about what to do if their children are being bullied, see **www.deewr.gov.au/schooling/nationalsafeschools/Pages/overview.aspx**. The framework is designed to provide, "… Australian schools with a vision and a set of guiding principles that assist school communities to take a proactive whole-school approach to developing effective student safety and wellbeing policies. This vision includes creating learning environments which are free from bullying, harassment, aggression and violence".

While what is called overt bullying (insulting and name calling, being physically attacked or having one's property vandalised) has been going on ever since children first went to school, the situation has grown worse and is more difficult to deal with because of the rise of more hidden forms of bullying associated with the new technologies. Cyber bullying (or covert bullying) involves students being victimised and threatened via SMS messaging or on social networking sites like chat-rooms, Facebook and YouTube. In a 2009 European study of teenagers using social media and the internet, over half of those surveyed in Norway said they had experienced cyber bullying, in Denmark the figure was 45% and in the UK 28% of those interviewed said they had been bullied on the internet.

Examples of cyber bullying include girls having embarrassing and compromising pictures circulated by ex-boyfriends, students being vilified and abused via SMS, students posting videos of other students being beaten and humiliated on YouTube and students sending threatening emails. Cyber bullying is especially dangerous as it can happen as quickly as posting on a website or sending an SMS message. Unlike being physically bullied (where you can sometimes simply walk away and that most often happens at school) cyber bullying can occur 24/7 and the results follow you wherever you go. Cyber bullying is also difficult for parents and teachers to uncover as a lot of what is occurring is out of sight and it can spread like wildfire across the internet or mobile network in a matter of seconds.

According to a Commonwealth study set up to investigate the problem, these new forms of bullying are far worse than the old ones. In a report called *Australia Covert Bullying Prevalence Study*, the authors state, "… covert bullying has the potential to result in more severe psychological, social, and mental health problems than overt bullying, and is not only more difficult for schools and parents to detect, but also has the capacity to inflict social isolation on a much broader scale than overt bullying".

What's to be done in the home?

Parents have a role to play to teach their children to respect and be civil to others and not to bully and intimidate those around them. As discussed in Chapter 5, if children have a strong moral compass then there is a much greater chance that they will be sympathetic and supportive, instead of being aggressive and violent. Learning to be compassionate is a strong antidote to wanting to victimise and hurt others. Even before kindergarten and pre-school, it is vital that young children are taught some basic but simple rules about how to behave. Examples include learning that violence and anger are unacceptable as well as counter-productive, respecting others and realising the value of already mentioned sayings like, "do unto others as you would have them do unto you".

Parents also need to be good role models and understand that how they treat one another and how they act in the home can have a significant impact on their children. It's understandable that if parents are rude and aggressive, both verbally and physically, then children grow up thinking that such behaviour is acceptable.

Those who have read Golding's *Lord of the Flies* will understand how children, free of restraint and adult authority, can be cruel and violent to another, with the weakest being most vulnerable and at risk of suffering. In addition to being taught that bullying is wrong, children, both when they are young and when becoming teenagers, need to be taught to be resilient, to have self-control and how to deal with challenges and confrontations.

Once again literature has a role to play. Stories like the *The Odyssey*, where Odysseus is forced to overcome adversity and danger on his return to his wife and home in Ithaca after the fall of Troy, tells us that it is possible to overcome great challenges and dangers. Tolkien's trilogy *The Lord of The Rings* also shows how unassuming heroes like Frodo and Sam can achieve great things through their own bravery, endurance and the help of one another. As noted by the Melbourne psychologist, Michael Carr-Gregg, "adversity doesn't always have to be negative". If you are confident and have self-esteem it is more difficult for others to bully and intimidate you.

While bullying is unacceptable, parents also need to understand that young children, like farmyard animals, are programmed to test one another out and to establish a pecking order either in the schoolyard or amongst friends. For children, an important part of growing up is testing yourself against others, realising when you have overstepped the line and learning to resolve your own problems.

Cyber bullying

Given the destructive influence and prevalence of cyber bullying it is also vital that parents do all they can to make sure that their children are both safe and not misusing the new technologies. Parents should:

- take computers out of children's bedrooms and put them in a place where use can be easily monitored,
- make sure computers have some kind of internet filter to block offensive and dangerous material,
- warn children about not sharing personal information, including photos and contact details,
- refuse to buy primary school age children a mobile phone – if they don't have one it cannot be misused,
- watch their children for signs of unusual or excessive computer and mobile phone use. Parents also need to be sensitive to any unusual or uncharacteristic behaviour that often occurs as a result of being a victim of bullying, such as becoming withdrawn, irritable, anti-social or depressed, and
- teach children about the rules and ethics of new ways of communicating like SMS messaging and being involved in chat-

rooms and other types of social networking sites. Children need to know that they can face fines, and even imprisonment, if they cyber bully others or help to circulate offensive photos, videos and other material that causes embarrassment and harm.

A valuable resource for parents that helps to deal with cyber bullying funded by the Australian Government is Cybersmart, found at http://www.cybersmart.gov.au/.

Working with schools

Parents need to work in partnership with their children's schools when it comes to bullying and make sure they do everything they can to support teachers. As already mentioned, anti-bullying strategies should begin in the home as teachers find it very frustrating and time consuming to have to deal with children who think it is OK to bully others and who have never been taught the difference between good and bad behaviour.

Across Australia, many education departments are doing all they can to help and support parents by giving advice, holding workshops and making information available. One example of such a partnership is the Queensland Government's Working together: a toolkit for parents to address bullying, see http://education.qld.gov.au/studentservices/behaviour/qsaav/index.html. The toolkit is designed to provide parents with, "practical tips on how to support their child should they experience or engage in bullying behaviour. It also provides information and strategies to assist parents in communicating with school staff should any concerns regarding bullying arise". Included in the toolkit is a series of videos by Michael Carr-Gregg, a Melbourne-based psychologist specialising in youth issues like bullying, self-esteem and developing resilience. (The first in the series of bullying videos can be found at http://www.youtube.com/watch?v=b597hE4k_ic). At the national level another website dedicated to addressing the bullying issue is one that was established in June 2002 called "Bullying No Way", found at http://www.bullyingnoway.com.au/.

Schools also develop their own anti-bullying strategies that generally involve clear guidelines about what constitutes acceptable and unacceptable behaviour, children's rights and responsibilities and the consequences students face if they bully, threaten or intimidate others. Parents need to make sure they know their child's school policy and do all they can to support it. At a minimum, anti-bullying strategies should involve:

- a whole school approach to bullying that is incorporated in the school's strategy plan along with associated issues like discipline and behaviour,
- a consistent approach that is supported and implemented by all teachers and that is communicated to students and parents,
- professional development to ensure that teachers are up to date with anti-bullying research and approaches that have proven to be effective elsewhere,
- workshops and seminars for parents and their children to discuss and learn about the issue,
- dealing with bullying issues in subjects like Health and Physical Education and English with a focus on teaching students about the consequences of bullying and developing skills such as conflict resolution and anger management,
- effective supervision of students before and after school and at recess and lunchtime to ensure that opportunities for bullying are minimised,
- designing effective procedures for dealing with bullying when it occurs (including communicating with parents and health professionals, where required), and
- evaluating the effectiveness of the school's anti-bullying strategies and including information about the issue in the school's annual report.

9

Parents, Teachers and Schools: It's a Partnership

As mentioned in Chapter 1, parents have a vital role to play in preparing their children for formal education. Teaching young children to respect authority and to be civil to other children, stimulating a child's curiosity and love of discovery, providing educational games and introducing them to children's story books, the alphabet and numbers are all needed to provide a solid foundation on which schools and teachers can build.

Parents also need to remember, though, that while the home is the first place where children start to learn and they have the primary responsibility to educate their children, teachers and schools are also vitally important. Education requires a partnership between parents and teachers as the overwhelming majority of students are at school for 12 years and for many this represents the most formative and important years before they become young adults.

Let teachers get on with their job

Years ago, children walked or rode their bikes to school and those parents that did accompany them left them at the school gate. Teachers were (and still are) highly qualified and respected professionals and most parents were happy to let them get on with the job of teaching their children, without interfering or closely monitoring what was going on. As a teacher, during the '70s and '80s, I only met parents twice a year, during parent/teacher nights, and I still remember those parents, generally fathers when talking about their sons, whose advice was if there was any trouble, just give him a clip over the ear. It was rare for parents to want to sit in on lessons, try to contact you to have a meeting at school or to phone about some incident that their child was worried about.

How times have changed! Parents no longer leave their children at the school gate and many, especially those with primary school age children and at the start of the new school year, expect to sit in on lessons and to have a say in what is to be taught. It's not unusual for teachers walking the corridor or while on yard duty to be confronted by a parent complaining about how their child is being unfairly treated (parents always take the child's side) or asking why their pet subject is not on the curriculum.

The new technologies are making matters a lot worse. Students now have mobiles and it's not uncommon, after being told off or punished by a teacher for doing something wrong, for a student to SMS his or her parent who soon arrives at the school defending the child. Giving teachers laptops and internet access sounds good in theory but, in those schools where parents have access to teachers' email addresses the teachers are bombarded with emails 24/7 and are expected to be at the parents' beck and call. So much for a quiet weekend!

When writing about helicopter parents, I mentioned that angry parent syndrome and the fact that many teachers are increasingly being intimidated and threatened by parents. In South Australia, the number of parents banned from schools, while relatively small, has doubled in two years and it's not unusual for teachers to ask for principals to be available during parent/teacher interviews as many parents become aggressive when told that their child is under-achieving or not putting in the required effort.

In NSW a number of schools have banned parents from entering the school without permission, and asked them to drop their children off at the school gate. To justify the bans, the head of the NSW Primary Principals Association, Jim Cooper, has been quoted as saying, "There are a number of parents across the state who sometimes can become a little aggressive" and, "We have to protect our staff and we have a responsibility for the safety and care of children. It becomes very difficult for the school but we have to appeal to the community to act appropriately".

10
Understanding Education Fads and Jargon

When it comes to education and how schools work, one of the most confusing things for parents and the most difficult to understand relates to education fads and jargon.

It's almost as though some teacher academics and schools want to make it impossible for parents to know what is going on with their child's education.

The first thing to understand is that education, like many other professions, is influenced by fads that come and go and that give the impression that schools are successful by keeping up to date with the latest trends. A lot of what happens in the classroom is also often couched in edubabble and jargon that often sounds impressive but does little to improve learning or raise standards.

Anyone who questions or fights against education fads and jargon is attacked as old-fashioned and out of touch.

The following is designed to cut through the jargon and help parents when they visit schools, talk to teachers and try to find out what is really going on, whether their child is learning successfully and whether the school is right for their child. It should also be said that while some fads are OK, when they take over the classroom and are treated as the only way to teach then students suffer.

(1) Assessment

During their time at school students will encounter many different types of assessment, ranging from their projects and work being assessed by the classroom teacher, to state, territory and Australia wide literacy and numeracy tests, to end-of-year, formal, competitive examinations. While many parents want traditional assessment, where students pass and fail, progressive teachers argue that failing students is bad for their self-esteem, that competition is unhealthy and that assessment should not be used to compare one student's performance against another.

(2) Child-centred learning

Instead of putting subjects like science, mathematics and history centre stage, and making sure that every student learns what teachers say is important, a child-centred approach argues that the spotlight must be on the child. In the classroom students decide what they want to learn, based on their interests and what they think is important, and teachers facilitate learning instead of taking charge and telling students what they should learn. The focus is on the world of the child and learning is made immediately relevant, attractive and accessible instead of students being made to learn what progressive teachers argue is old-fashioned and of no immediate use.

(3) Constructivist

A term used by progressive teachers to argue, instead of being taught, that children learn best by taking control of their own learning. Similar to 'discovery learning', the belief is that it is best for students to negotiate what they learn, to learn at their own pace and not to be taught in a formal, more structured way. A constructivist classroom is generally an open one where students work in groups, teachers facilitate and where there is little, if any, reliance on memorisation, rote learning or whole class teaching. Whole language and fuzzy maths are based on a constructivist approach.

(4) Deferred success

Many schools and teachers argue that the 'F' word should be banned from the classroom and that work should not be marked using red pens. Alternatives to marking children's work out of 10 or using A to E is to use descriptions like "deferred success", "consolidating" and "not yet achieved". As a result of this sensitive, new-age approach to assessment many children go through school never being told they have failed. Children think they are doing OK, when in fact many are going backwards and leave school unable to cope with the next stage of learning or the real world where success and failure are facts of life.

(5) Developmental learning

Whereas a traditional approach to education expects students at each year level to master what is being taught before they move on to the next level, progressive teachers argue that learning is developmental. By this they mean that students learn in their own way and at their own speed. As a result, worried parents are told not to worry if their child is falling behind other students and that he or she will soon grow into it! The fact is that many don't and students leave primary school unable to read and write and many, after finishing secondary school, have to do remedial courses at university. In the US, many states no longer allow students to be automatically promoted (what Americans term 'getting rid of social progression') and, instead, make students attend summer school or stay down a year until they reach the required standard and catch up with their peers.

(6) Edubabble

Education should be about communicating clearly, simply and directly and avoiding gobbledygook and jargon. Such is not the case and following is a short guide translating some of the current jargon:

- *Knowledge navigators/digital natives* – students.
- *Facilitators/guides by the side* – teachers.
- *Collaborative, negotiated, life-long learning* – education.
- *Autonomous learners* – children.
- *Pedagogically sensitive learning space* – classroom.

(7) Facilitators/guides by the side

The more traditional style of learning involves teachers taking control of the classroom, acting as authority figures and teaching. Across the English-speaking world, including England, the US, Australia and New Zealand and beginning in the late '60s, this more direct approach to teaching was attacked as old-fashioned and bad for students. Under the banner of progressive education the argument is that children learn best when the teacher acts as a friend and fellow learner and lets students manage their own learning. Ignored is the research that suggests that the more direct, formal methods of teaching are the most effective. Boys, in particular, need a structured classroom where teachers, instead of being guides by the side, control and monitor what is happening from the front of the room, maintain discipline and give the class clear instructions on what they should be doing.

(8) Fuzzy maths

The more traditional approach to mathematics involves memorising multiplication tables, mental arithmetic (no calculators) and mastering basic algorithms like long division. Fuzzy maths or 'real world' maths adopts many of the characteristics of progressive education, such as cooperative learning, group learning, teachers as facilitators and relating learning to 'real-life' situations. Ignored is the research about how children learn that tells us that rote learning and memorisation skills are essential if higher order skills are to be acquired.

(9) Life-long learning

A slogan used by progressive teachers when arguing that traditional approaches to teaching are old-fashioned and out-of-date. Instead of teachers teaching in a systematic and structured way, standing at the front of the class and controlling what students learn, the argument is that students need to be 'independent' and 'autonomous' learners. Teachers advocating life-long learning usually adopt a constructivist approach, based on the belief that students have to be prepared for life outside the classroom. Ignored is that schools, in may ways, are not like the outside world and that unless students are taught properly during their time in the classroom they will leave school with low levels of literacy and numeracy and unable to cope.

(10) Open classrooms

The more traditional classroom is one where the whiteboard (or blackboard) is at the front of the room, students sit in rows or a u-shape and classes are divided into year levels with the one teacher in charge. Open classrooms are the opposite, they are classrooms where two to three year levels work together, teachers become facilitators and instead of whole class teaching, children work in groups and take control of their own learning. Open classrooms are often noisy and it is hard for students, especially boys, to concentrate and get on with their work.

(11) Outcomes-based education (OBE)

During the '80s and '90s OBE became the dominant model for education in the US, New Zealand, Australia, England and South Africa. In deciding what schools should teach, OBE adopts a progressive approach, one that is child-centred, process driven, politically correct and non-competitive. The details telling teachers what to teach are often vague, ambiguous and hard to measure and there are so many of them that teachers drown in the detail. While popular during the '90s, most countries that experimented with OBE no longer advocate the model as it led to a dumbed down curriculum, falling standards and stressed, over-worked teachers.

(12) Personalised learning

Similar to child-centred learning that was popular during the late 60s and '70s, personalised learning puts the child centre stage. Teachers act as "guides by the side" and learning is based on the child's interests, needs and immediate environment. Personalised learning also relies heavily on new technologies on the basis that teachers can be replaced by computers and the internet.

(13) Political correctness

PC teachers argue that education must be used to change society and to teach children politically correct views about the environment, multiculturalism, feminism, peace studies and sexuality. Examples include: European settlement described as an invasion, schools refusing to celebrate Christmas as it might offend non-Christians, and Western civilisation being attacked as corrupt, misogynistic, homophobic and racist.

(14) Process learning

Subjects like English, mathematics, science and history are made up of important content that teachers teach and students are expected to learn. Process learning argues that content is secondary and not as important as learning *how* to learn. Using computers and the internet to find and gather information, on whatever topic, and learning how to work in teams are good examples of process learning. Ignored is that cultural literacy depends on being taught subjects like history and literature and that such subjects have essential content that all children deserve to be taught.

(15) Progressive education

An approach to education that took off in the mid-to-late 60s and early '70s across the English-speaking world as a reaction against more traditional approaches to learning. This was a time of Vietnam moratoriums, Woodstock, the counter-culture, feminism and the civil rights movement. In classrooms young, progressive teachers argued for community schools, a child-centred view of education, getting rid of syllabuses, inspectors and examinations, and teaching students how to radically change society by adopting politically correct beliefs. Progressive teachers argued that *what* students learned is secondary to developing skills like working in groups, finding information and learning how to research a topic.

(16) Rote learning

Progressive teachers attack rote learning as learning to recite useless facts and children being made to parrot information in a mechanical way. Examples include: memorising times tables, the dates of important historical events, learning poems and ballads off by heart and doing mental arithmetic. Ignored is the research that suggests, especially when children are young, that memorising and rote learning are very important if children are going to succeed later on in school.

(17) Students as knowledge navigators / life long learners

Instead of teachers being in charge and telling children what to learn, many schools put the children centre stage. Beginning in England, Australia, New Zealand and US in the late '60s, the idea is that if children control their learning and decide for themselves what they want to do they will be better motivated and get more enjoyment out of being at school. As a result of computers and the internet, instead of teachers teaching the class as a whole and telling children what they should learn, children are free to search the internet, doing their own projects and research. Ignored is that children waste a lot of time on the internet and nothing can ever replace the expertise and skill of teachers.

(18) Whole language

Advocates of whole language argue that learning to read is as easy and natural as learning to speak. Instead of teaching phonics and phonemic awareness, progressive teachers argue that children should "look and guess" or work out the meaning of words by their context. In the jargon of whole language children are "immersed in a rich language environment" and there is little attempt to learn how to read by dividing words into their letter/sound combinations, to memorise spelling lists or to learn correct grammar. Boys are especially disadvantaged by whole language and the fact that many students leave primary school unable to read and write is result of the whole language fad. Many children are also labelled as dyslexic or having eye trouble when the real problem is that they have never been properly taught how to read.

11
Conclusion

The Persian poet Kahlil Gibran, in his poem *On Children*, tells parents that while they might like to control their children and direct their path in life, children have a life and a destiny of their own.

Gibran begins his poem as follows:

Your children are not your children.
They are the sons and daughters of Life's longing for itself.
They come through you but not from you,
And though they are with you yet they belong not to you.

In one sense, Gibran is right. Children are born with a unique personality, physique and temperament as any mother or father appreciates. It's also true that children very early in life develop a mind and character of their own and don't always follow the road set out by their parents.

At the same time, it is wrong to think that parents and family are without influence and that children are autonomous and free to set their own direction in life. In his poem, Gibran suggests such is the case when he writes:

You are the bows from which your children
as living arrows are sent forth.
The archer sees the mark upon the path of the infinite,
and He bends you with His might
that His arrows may go swift and far.
Let your bending in the archer's hand be for gladness;
For even as He loves the arrow that flies,
so He loves also the bow that is stable.

In many ways having children is far more momentous and significant than getting married or establishing a long-term relationship. As parents, there is no greater responsibility than bringing new life into the world and ensuring that children are loved, comforted, fed and clothed and given a balanced, sound and enriching education.

As stated in Gibran's poem – you are the bows from which your children are launched into life.

www.ingramcontent.com/pod-product-compliance
Lightning Source LLC
Chambersburg PA
CBHW031607110426
42742CB00037B/1325